Unforgettable Memories

Thelma "Pixie" Williamson

Edited By: Todd Larson & Sherma Bowe

School photos taken by Ahvia Campbell Photographer for Ministry of Education and Technical and Vocational Training, Nassau, Bahamas.

Cover Design By: Jaquay Adderley

Photos of Cover Design By Fabian Photography at Montague Beach, Nassau, Bahamas.

Acknowledgements

My unceasing gratitude goes to my extraordinary mother, my loving husband Howard; my motivating "iron sharpening iron" daughters and sons-in-law, inspiring siblings, extended family, friends, outstanding primary (elementary), junior, secondary high schools, distinguished college facilitators, and supportive classmates for an incredible life journey thus far!

Special commendations to Atlantic College in Nassau, New Providence, in the Commonwealth of the Bahamas, including my phenomenal Advance College Writing Facilitator Mrs. Lily Moxey for stirring my dormant literary juices, above all, inspiring, motivating, and challenging me to write at a higher academic level.

Mrs. Sherma Bowe, a 40-year retired veteran Language Arts public school teacher with the Ministry of Education in the Bahamas, as well as a Christian minister, thank you for your loyal support and great confidence in my endeavors.

A special thanks to the Ministry of Education and Technical and Vocational Training, Nassau, Bahamas for the use of the photos of the various schools in this book.

All honor, glory, and praise to the Holy Spirit from whom all wisdom, knowledge, understanding, revelation, and truth flows.

"Oh that my words were now written! Oh that they were printed in a book! That they were graven with an iron pen and lead in the rock forever!"

(Job 19:23-24 King James Version).

I believe that one of the most enjoyable, memorable achievements in life is to have created unforgettable memories, as well as to have shared extraordinary experiences with people, places, and things that you genuinely, passionately love!

A Message to the Reader

My life thus far has been an amazing, indelible journey of impactful unforgettable childhood memories, including cognitive experiences that are forever embedded in my brain and the depths of my throbbing heart.

Admittedly, after six decades of my life, I am similar to clay, having been firmly pressed, rolled, and molded now into a lovely, unique, gifted, influential, valuable, phenomenal sculptured human vessel of honor! I am continuously polished for my Creator's purposeful use in our modern, high-tech, diverse global world.

I am truly convinced that it makes no difference if our unforgettable memories were pleasurable or devastatingly painful, because when diligently and critically analyzed, at least a minuscule amount of positivity could always be discovered.

Remarkably, when armed with such revelation and truth, we can be propelled forward to further continuous development, in addition to never-ending maturity.

I encourage you, as an airline pilot would, to click on your engine of life, gracefully taxi on your runway of adventure and discovery, next lift off, soaring like an eagle high above the gloomy thunderous clouds, brilliant lightnings, and breezy winds of the fray to victoriously accomplish your God-ordained prophetic dreams, visions, goals, purposes, and destinies!

Table of Contents

Chapter 1
Some Recollections Never Fade

The deep, soothing, serenading baritone voice of the jazz singer bellowed the lyrics "Unforgettable" through the tranquil airwaves in my family's green-and-white-trimmed house in Nassau, New Providence, Bahamas at Brougham Street off East Street.

Fully aware that we were home alone because our mother, Mrs. Thelma—my namesake—had gone early to work, my second eldest sibling, Beverley—nicknamed Barbie, a sweet Cadbury-chocolate-skinned, medium-height young adult with short afro hair who always believed she was large and in charge—dashed past me like a coyote to restart our old-fashioned brown record player!

I concluded over the years that Barbie was either madly in love with a young man or devastatingly heartbroken, since she replayed this one song like a broken record every weekend. Both Barbie and my eldest sister, Beryl, were literal freaks of similar golden-oldies songs, hence like the helpless sacrificial lamb I had been brainwashed into being from a youngster. I was always petrified to turn the record player dial lower, so I had to simply suck it up.

Suddenly, oblivious to me, Barbie stopped cleaning the house, and then quickly wiped her hands on her white apron, next, skillfully placed the record player's dial needle on the large black circular record album to restart her golden oldie "Unforgettable" once again. This time she turned the record player volume dial to its hollering maximum. The walls seemed to vibrate as the lyrics serenaded through the entire house.

I hid while covering my ears with my tiny hands to peer back into the kitchen while Barbie, as if mesmerized, closed her eyes tightly, threw her head back to inhale a deep breath, and slowly exhaled. Next, she enclosed her right hand into a tight-balled fist like a microphone and lifted it to her mouth to sing in her usual loud, off-key tone in her customarily shrieking voice. Shaking my head from side to side, I giggled quietly, questioning why in heaven's name Barbie believed she could sing melodiously. On several occasions I overheard her informing other family members that I was simply jealous of her singing talent. In utter disbelief, I concluded that not even Nancy Drew could solve my sister Barbie's complex mysterious singing problem.

As the golden-oldie song continued to play, surprisingly, unexpectedly out of the blue, Barbie transformed into an irrational woman and quickly grabbed our yellow, slender, four-foot-tall kitchen broom standing helplessly alone in a corner for a romantic waltz dance partner on our kitchen floor! Stunned, I watched as both Barbie and Mr. Yellow Broom rhythmically stepped forward, backward and sideward repeatedly, as if they were intimate lovers.

My tiny eyes strained wide open like huge saucers in my sockets, totally transfixed on this pair. As if watching a movie, my little head tilted in all directions as Barbie and Mr.

Yellow Brown twisted, twirled, swayed, and tap-danced harmoniously, synchronizing their movements to the beat of the music. Eventually, the instrumental music segued into a more drooling, caressing, intoxicating, and baptizing tone while Barbie tightly clutched Mr. Yellow Broom to her bosom in a suffocating, forever loving embrace.

The music stopped, but Barbie and Mr. Yellow Broom continued to waltz slowly around our kitchen ballroom dance floor. Barbie, now breathless and perspiring profusely, finally collapsed into a chair while her hands dropped, and Mr. Yellow Broom fell to the kitchen floor with a loud *thud, thud!* My tiny eyes popped out of my sockets as Barbie's face glowed brilliantly like an angel from heaven with a broad smile carved on her face. I giggled quietly, enthralled with these amazing, unforgettable moments. Suddenly, similar to Scotty on *Star Trek*, I requested to be beamed back to planet Earth from the time-zone era of the early seventies.

After I aroused to consciousness, I blinked my eyes several times and stared at our clock in my living room, its dials set to my present date and time, Wednesday, July 7, 2021, 4 p.m. I laughed once again, having recalled such pleasurable, memorable collections of my unorthodox, comical "Bahamas Got Talent" nominee and likewise undisputed *Gong Show* champion, my beloved sister, Barbie!

It is amazing, notwithstanding I am now an adult woman, yet I can remember as if it were yesterday the deep, soothing, serenading baritone voice and lyrics of Mr. Incomparable Nat forever cemented in my brain and soul. Furthermore, there are other remarkable cognitive unforgettable memories of my memorable life of my primary, junior, plus senior high school days which are etched forever in my brain, soul, and spirit!

Chapter 2
The Journey Begins

Though it is very difficult to recall every single detail of my life and primary (elementary) school days from grades one to six, for the most part there were some experiences that were simply unforgettable memories!

I was informed by my eldest sister Beryl that many years after the death of our mother's husband and while a widow, she met my father and eventually became pregnant with me. When I got older, Beryl frequently reminded me of our mother's shocking pregnancy, my premature birth, and months of hospitalization. Beryl recanted that when she and my other siblings saw me for the first time after my discharge from hospital they were shocked at my physical size and she stated, *"I looked like a Pixie"* which eventually became my nickname and has stuck throughout my life. Surprisingly, I am no longer petite but have grown tall similar to the height of my parents. Despite not having a close relationship with my biological father because of my parents' personal issues, and complicated by his death due to an illness at forty-six years; nevertheless I remained optimistic, focused on my futuristic personal and educational goals.

At five years old, during the fall semester my loving mother woke me at 6 am; as a swarm of butterflies fluttered in my stomach. I was ecstatic with jubilation to commence my first day of schooling at Naomi Blatch Primary School! After a bath my mother assisted in adorning me in my neatly pressed school uniform—an aqua-blue jumper, an aqua-and-white-checkered Peter Pan collar blouse, aqua-blue socks, and my shining black polished Clarke's shoes. Every strain of my hair was *"straightened"* with a hot comb, as well as beautifully decorated with aqua ribbons and white bumbles. Lovingly, my mother whispered, *"My baby, you look beautiful and smart."* Instantly, my self-esteem was blasted to the moon making me feel greatly loved and very special!

Determined that I not arrive late to school, I quickly ate my breakfast. Afterwards, my mother quickly grasped my tiny hand as we walked briskly from our home. My first sight of Naomi Blatch Primary School was a neatly painted, blue-trimmed white two-story concrete stone structure with classrooms and offices, in addition to two one-story structures. Our entire campus was enclosed with a strong, thick, silver chain-link fence and high concrete walls.

At its front entrance stood a Goliath-sized gentleman adorned in a white shirt and black trousers. His deep-throated voiced bellowed like thunder above our heads, *"I am Security Officer Mr. Johnson. Welcome to Naomi Blatch Primary School the best little school in the Bahamas!"* I smiled, reassured I would be protected.

Our school principal was Mrs. Saunders, a tall, articulate, stern-faced woman who frequently patrolled our school campus similar to a drill sergeant. Thankfully, I rarely visited my principal's immaculate office, except to conduct prefect duties in grade level six. Unbelievably, it was on these few occasions I heard Mrs. Saunders speak pleasantries and saw her crack a smile. I was convinced our principal visited a beauty salon every weekend, because her hair was always well groomed in a high-pinned twisted bun. Comically, it looked similar to a bird's nest with tons of hairspray that kept it firmly in its position.

My schooling from grades one to five seemed to move swiftly by. I recall my grade five and six teachers reinforce information about eating nutritious meals, personal hygiene, and puberty. As a result, I adjusted quite well when my physical body began to gradually develop.

In grades five and six I was more academically focused, as well as more responsible. I began to understand my distinct purpose for school attendance, hence I decided to make the most of every single day there. I developed an intense passion for and loving dedication to school attendance and my studies. My grades of A and B not only increased but became consistent each term. Incredibly, throughout my primary-school six years I was never ill, tardy, or absent. I believed it was because of my extraordinary, determined, visionary mother,

Mrs. Thelma, who envisioned a higher educational status of achievement for me above her own.

Chapter 3
Best Time of School

Every day, precisely at noon at Naomi Blatch Primary School, my stomach growled *grrr, grrr* as if a hungry bear to signal like a clock my favorite occasion—lunch time!

Quickly we recited our daily lunch prayer:

"Thank you for the world so sweet,
Thank you for the food we eat,
Thank you for the birds that sing,
Thank you, God, for everything.
For health and strength and
Daily bread we thank Thee, Lord Amen"
(Cited by Lisa Lou of Pinterest (no date).

I raced from my classroom as fast as a lightning bolt to Ms. Bain a lunch vendor's stall. She was a beloved, plump, jovial lady.

My eyes twinkled then popped out of my head as I gazed greedily at her well-stocked stall with my favorite food, drinks, and snacks. Of course, this was decades ago, but oh, how modern times have transformed protocols to empower schools to become educators of healthy nutritious meals and lifestyles.

As students shoved and stepped on my tiny toes, I shouted, *"Ms. Bain! Ms. Bain! Could I please have one-dollar chicken wings and French fries?"* In an instant my food was handed to me on a tiny white plate and money snatched from my small hands. Hastily, Ms. Bain replied, *"Thank you! Next?"*

My classmate Maureen and I found a nice cool shaded area under a leafy tree on the small playground to sit and eat our lunches. I quickly buried my head in my food plate, greedily devouring Ms. Bain's delicious fare. I smacked my lips including fingers dry.

"Wow!" I exclaimed. Ms. Bain's lunch was most definitely off the chain, as I stared down at my empty plate. I placed my tiny hands on my tummy, and then smiled a broad upper-two-front-row toothless grin. Once my

tummy was filled, I was most definitely ecstatically exuberant!

After lunch, my female classmates and I enjoyed games such as Hopscotch and Twee-lee-lee. During The Ring Play game, we made a wide circle and clapped our hands as each girl stepped forward with hands on her waistline rocking from side to side while we sang the lyrics,

"There's a brown girl in the ring, tra la la la la.
There's a brown girl in the ring, tra la la la la la.
Brown girl in the ring tra la la la la
And she looks like a sugar in a plum, plum, plum.
So, show me your motion, tra la la la la.
Come on show me your motion tra la la la la la.
Show me your motion, tra la la la la.
She looks like a sugar in a plum, plum, plum."

I disliked when our male classmates congregated to play Pork Me. Instantly, my eyes filled with tears, since I was usually smacked with a tennis ball, because I was a snail-paced runner. The after effect was a stingingly painful sensation on my skin. More often than not, when lunch recess ended, most of us were unrecognizable after being immersed in white soil from our school's playing field. My immaculate uniform, well-groomed hair and expensive black Clarke's shoes were in a deplorable state!

Acutely knowledgeable about my mother's stern rules of tidiness, along with her giving me a sandwich to take to school instead of lunch money for Ms. Bain's cuisine, I would race to my school's bathroom to use tons of water to erase from my clothing or hair any evidence of being an accessory to a crime. I do not think I was deceptive to my loving mother, only having long-lasting, superb, enjoyable fun, not forgetting creating long lasting unforgettable memories!

Chapter 4
School Drama!

On this rare day the bell rang very early at Naomi Blatch Primary School to end my beloved lunch time! *"You guessed right!"* As a loyal customer I was already towing a line standing stoically behind only two classmates at Ms. Bain's stall to place my standard lunch order.

Stunningly, the bell rang again. Students froze for a few minutes, screamed, next darted to their individual classrooms, their heads cramped with questions!

Ms. Taylor instructed everyone to settle down as we watched through the windows as an ambulance arrived and medical persons rushed to a classroom. Thankfully, before the bell rang at 3 p.m. for our school dismissal, Ms. Taylor reassured us the person's medical condition had improved. I was grateful that this incident did not end tragically.

Naomi Blatch Primary School's annual Harvest Thanksgiving and Christmas services were conducted at St. Barnabas Anglican Church opposite the school's premises. Students were neatly dressed in our uniforms. I was thrilled to get a break from our academic routine to experience something unique. During these special occasions I was introduced to the singing of beautiful hymns such as "Praise to the Lord the Almighty," *"Now Thank We All Our God," "All Things Bright and Beautiful," "O Little Town of Bethlehem,"* and *"Away in a Manager,"* which are forever ingrained in my mind, heart, soul, and spirit.

Never in my wildest dreams would I consider the lyrics, music, and singing of hymns so relevant, impactful, inspirational, and beneficial in my life until decades later, such as when I was sick, the surgery of my youngest daughter Christina, and after the deaths of my beloved mother Thelma, my father John, and my sister Patricia. Hymns provided great solace, peace, faith, hope, and courage for me to not give up but continue to trust God and move forward.

At our school's annual Harvest Thanksgiving services, we collected and donated tons of fruits and vegetables—pumpkins, watermelons, bananas, tangerines, sugar apples, oranges, sweet potatoes, cassava, sugar canes, avocado pears, coconuts etc. to be distributed to charitable organizations.

Every school day at 3 p.m. after the school bell rang for dismissal, not missing a beat, Ms. Taylor would walk ahead of her little darlings like a proud peacock to the front gate. Resembling obedient soldiers, my classmates and I marched along in a straight line lifting our feet upward and downward behind Ms. Taylor with our fingers on our lips. Meanwhile, our dependable parents and guardians stood patiently outside the gate to welcome us.

The completion of my primary school education was our sixth-grade graduation. I was thrilled to have my mother and siblings, mot forgetting Barbie in attendance. They all cheered loudly for me as I received academic awards for English Language, Mathematics, Social Studies, Reading, and Religious Knowledge. With immense joy I welcomed my summer recess for all my hard work.

My beloved mother never a procrastinator for anything, commenced early preparation for my transfer to junior high school by ensuring our seamstress Mrs. Josephine a short stature, friendly lady sewed my new blue, yellow and red-striped plaid skirts. I was not bold enough to question my mother, or Mrs. Josephine who measured my skirt length below my knees and loosely fitted as if I was a nun.

I stared up at my tall mother as she embarrassingly emphasized to Mrs. Josephine that my uniforms needed to last for the entire three years of junior high school, which indeed prophetically occurred.

Thankfully, my primary school days were void of violence, fighting and bullying. Instead, I was overwhelmed with great joy, excitement, and serenity. I smiled broadly as my mind strolled down memory lane and reflected on the truthful words of Security Officer Mr. Johnson decades ago, "Welcome to Naomi Blatch Primary School the best little school in the Bahamas!" I concur.

Chapter 5
Church Experiences

While attending Naomi Blatch Primary School in the sixth grade my cousins Judy, Sandra, Betty, and Janet visited my home in transit to their church's Girls Auxiliary (G. A.) meetings for girls ages five to seventeen years old.

Meetings were conducted every Wednesday in the afternoon after school hours at the Transfiguration Baptist Church. They extended an invitation to my mother and obtained consent for me to attend along with them.

Several months later, my cousins informed my mother of their relocation to another community and their inability to accompany me any longer. My mother agreed for me to continue attending the meetings, but instructed me not to talk to anyone in transit or stop anywhere. For years I followed my mother's advice and experienced no mishaps. I enjoyed attending G.A. because we met new friends, recited memory verses and poetries, participated in bible quizzes, spelling and bible drill competitions, church services, socials, and trips to the island of Eleuthera to conduct Vacation Bible School.

I was elected to serve as an officer in different capacities including president and secretary. These opportunities boosted my knowledge, as well as my confidence, boldness, and oratorical skills to speak publicly and interact socially with diverse people. On special occasions and our yearly anniversary days we would parade through our community streets adorned in our green tam caps, white blouses, yellow scarfs, green skirts, white tennis shoes, and white socks. We were accompanied by the Royal Ambassadors Band which provided loud, energetic, rhythmic, and melodious music in which I tremendously enjoyed!

Eventually, I became actively involved in the church's youth choir, youth fellowship group, and Sunday School Department for many years which enhanced my leadership.. skills in every facet of my life. One of my G. A. leaders and mentors was Rev. Sherma Bowe. My Pastor Rev. Dr. Garnet King, Rev. Basil Johnson, and Rev. Brazil McDonald were all positive male role models in my life. Decades later I met my husband Howard who was a public school teacher and pastor.

After our marriage, I became a member of the Robinson Morris African Methodist Episcopal Church and currently serve as an Iterant Elder and Associate Minister. I also serve as Bible Discovery Hour/Sunday School Superintendent, Bible Study Teacher, and Bahamas Conference Secretary for the Women in Ministry.

Undoubtedly, the Christian church community continues to be a lifelong strong pillar of teaching, guidance, inspiration, influence, and empowerment for my personal and spiritual life. Thankfully, I have no regrets, only unforgettable memories!

Chapter 6
S. C. McPherson Sharks

I was awe struck at the first sight of S. C. McPherson Junior High School, which daunted in comparison to my tiny-sized Naomi Blatch Primary School.

S. C. McPherson Junior High School was a massive, white-trimmed, blue-painted structure with numerous classrooms to accommodate about nine hundred students plus staff! The Bahamian government provided daily bus transit for students in my vicinity. Throughout my three years of enrollment, I was a very quiet person but remained focused academically, thus was assigned to every top grade level.

My outstanding junior high school days were largely due to my unique classmates, incredible administrators, teachers, and support staff. My favorite teacher Ms. Inspiration taught me History and Mrs. Tony a wide-eyed, tall, slim-built, fair-complexioned, soft-spoken lady who resembled a model taught English Language. I recalled Mrs. Tony's husband religiously picked her up at 4 p.m. in his red sports car and was always dressed debonairly, being a proprietor of a renowned men's fashion store.

Our physical education teacher, Mr. Miller, was a stern, short-statured, muscular gentleman who never accepted trivial excuses from students. Once I accidentally forgot to pack my Physical Education uniform, along with a few other students, and Mr. Miller instructed us to exercise and play softball in our school uniforms. After that day, I learnt a valuable lesson to be more responsible. The following week, I was adorned beautifully in my short blue pants and blue Wahoo sports shirt for P.E.

During my final eighth and ninth-grade terms I decided to choose as an elective subject the arts and drama. I became affiliated with our school's drama club and choir, both of which I immensely enjoyed. I smiled broadly as heartwarming unforgettable memories flooded my mind.

Notwithstanding, my singing in the choir was short lived, I remained committed to the drama club. Shockingly, our drama club instructor selected me to perform in a premiere role in our school production and mime to a song entitled *"Naughty Johnny"* written by Bahamian songwriter, artist, and cartoonist Eddie Minnis.

I learnt that miming is a most intriguing, but grueling challenge because it demands great skill and talent. The actor or actress does not speak, but uses theatrical interpretive body language, facial expressions, and physical actions to convey information through a character to the audience.

I portrayed the mother of a naughty boy named Johnny who was left at home to monitor a pot on a stove but instead went to play outdoors. Unfortunately, a fire erupted and totally destroyed their home. This was a revolutionary experience for me to accept, a shy and reserved student, but I lacked the courage to say no to my drama club instructor.

After numerous drama rehearsals during lunchtime and after school, I believed I was ready for "lights, camera, action". Surprisingly, on the scheduled date of our school's drama production the school's auditorium was jam-packed with exuberant students, teachers, and support staff, all geared up to enjoy authentic native Bahamian cultural songs, dance, poetry, drama, junkanoo, rake-and-scrape music. After my act was announced, the curtains were drawn to reveal a stage with various different scenes. The audience laughed hilariously after viewing me dressed in my mother's oversized colorful clothing, a white apron, straw hat, and lengthy black wig! Instantly, all my fears, nervousness and anxieties vanished into thin air when Eddie Minnis' rhythmic, pulsating music, along with his comical Bahamian dialect words, blasted through the auditorium cited from Lyrics Box (2021):

"Whoy, whoy, whoy,
I sorry fer you, boy,
What yer mar ger do
When she find out bout you?
Boy, people whoy, whoy

On the next side of the ocean,
Whoy, whoy, whoy,
Dey ger hear the commotion
And you ger need surgical operation
When she finish with you!"

When Johnny mar gon in town
Before she leave she say
Yeah Johnny watch the pot
Don't let it get too hot.
But as she turn away yeah
Johnny gone go play
He gar live to regret this day.

Well the cat jump through the window
Knock the pot off the stove
The wind brow the fire and make it burn
much higher.The fire catch the curtain, the
curtain catch the roof and Johnny mar
clapboard house burn down.

Refrain:
Ooohhh Naughty Johnny, oh Naughty
Johnny
Ooohhh Naughty Johnny, oh Naughty
Johnny

The entire audience erupted exuberantly with boisterous loud shouts, screams and laughter! Dramatically, I forgot about myself and was engrossed in my character role as Johnny's authoritative mother. Skillfully I moved around the stage, commanding the attention of the audience by placing my hands on my waistline and pointing my finger at little mischievous Johnny to obey my instructions. I constantly transformed my facial expressions; including physical bodily actions to effectively suit each lyric, context, and scene as Eddie Minnis' Bahamian dialect rhythmic song continue to blast through the auditorium:

"When Johnny mar come back home,
All she found was cinder.
She get the whole story from a neighbor named Miss Pinder.
She fall on she knees and say,
'Yeah if I have my way that boy ger live to regret dis day.'
She look under the floor,
She look in the bushes,
She look in one ole car, what leave long side the road.
She ask all the neighbors, but all they could

say was
Naughty Johnny he went dat way."

Refrain:
Ooohhh Naughty Johnny, oh Naughty Johnny
Ooohhh Naughty Johnny, oh Naughty Johnny.

I fell on my knees and searched through the various on-stage props also inquired from on stage actors the whereabouts of naughty Johnny. When Eddie Minnis' song finally ended, the entire audience rose to their feet in a thunderous rousing applause accompanied with loud shrieking screams and roars of my name: "Go, Thelma! Go, Thelma!"

As the stage curtain flowed downwards my drama instructor ran toward me with excited congratulatory exclamations of my stunning Oscar-caliber performance! I felt as if a newborn baby chick had just cracked out of its shell. This was indeed a self-defining unforgettable moment for me. While my outward personality remained quiet and reserved throughout the reminder of my entire junior high school years, my inward self-confidence and self-esteem stood tall as giants! I was being brewed into a quiet storm eventually to be reckoned with.

Our graduation ceremony took place in the school auditorium. We all looked stunningly beautiful in our school uniforms. Giant, tall, medium, and tiny-sized trophies stood elegantly on tables with white tablecloths for all conscientious, diligent students to receive. In my opinion, most of my classmates were focused and determined to succeed academically. I graduated with a diploma and received awards, certificates in English Language, Literature and Biology, in addition to achieving ten Bahamas Junior Certificates (BJC). Once again, my motto had triumphed: *"Hard work pays off!"*

Chapter 7
A. F. Adderley Tigers

My final three years of public school education were at A. F. Adderley Senior High School.

My scholarly principal was Mrs. Cooper a short-statured, plump, and polite, but stern lady. I believe my remarkable secondary high school days were unforgettable because of my exceptional classmates, administrators, educators, and support staff. I was not only taught academics but character, moral and spiritual values, including life coping skills.

Mrs. Taylor was a tall, fair-skinned, medium built humorous lady who taught both English Language and Literature classes with meticulous skill and precision. Her teaching sessions were never dull, but lively and provocative as she was ever so poetic and educating about *Romeo and Juliet, The Tempest,* and *The Sheldon Book of Verse.*

Also inspiring for me was two of my classmates: Philip, now an international banker who is fluent in Spanish, and Edward, now an industrial engineer employed at BORCO in Freeport, Grand Bahama in the Bahamas. Their intelligence, diligent study habits, and superb communication skills highly motivated me to follow suit to achieve similar academic successes.

I was overjoyed when I successfully achieved four General Certificate Education O Levels (GCE) and was chosen along with our school "head girl," or class president Charmaine as the top female students to represent the school at an awards ceremony. I was infused with tremendous courage, confidence, and diligence to continue to strive for excellence.

Our graduation was held in our large school gymnasium. All graduates looked radiant as angels, adorned in glistening white graduation robes, caps, and green satin sashes. Suddenly, reality struck me as I realized our paths were about to split into separate directions possibly not seeing some persons ever again. I experienced an emotional roller-coaster ride of euphoric highs of excitement, joys, laughter, and expectations, and then a quick, steep downward spiral of fears, concerns, and sadness.

My mother, brothers and sisters screamed as I paraded down the long, wide stage to receive my diploma and awards. My principal, Mrs. Cooper smiled proudly whilst grasping my hand in a firm congratulatory handshake.

I smiled proudly as I received academic awards for the High School Diploma, Honor Roll, English Language, English Literature, History, and Religious Knowledge. Tears flowed as I whispered to myself, "Thelma, you did it—your final walk on a twelve-year journey of basic primary, junior and secondary high school education!" Quickly I shook myself, as this was no time for tears, only celebration! Smiling broadly, I poised myself along with my best friend Rhonda and another classmate Sandy for pictures. "Smile" my brother Johnnie shouted as he snapped his small Polaroid camera. "Click, click, click!"

In conclusion, I summarized my entire twelve years of public school education from my beloved sister Barbie's favorite song: *"Unforgettable!"* Indisputably, my primary, junior, and senior high school days had created unforgettable memories! I was thrilled to move onto the next chapter of my life. I prayerfully contemplated the career paths possibly of teaching, policing, or nursing. Finally, I filled out an application form and was accepted into the Bahamas government Registered Nursing program. I served the Ministry of Health for twenty four years then moved onto another incredible chapter of my life!

The author's graduation photo.

Chapter 8
Retraced Footsteps into New Frontiers

In the face of the shocking Coronavirus (COVID-19) pandemic, it was both nostalgic and a most notable experience for me when I revisited the site of my beloved alma mater Naomi Blatch Primary School on Thursday 20, May 2021.

Childhood thoughts flooded my head as I parked my car then embarked. I literally froze for a few minutes as I stared at the two-story stone structure, now painted in mustard-trimmed green, standing stoically like a Bahamian historical monument having weathered decades of hurricanes. Unchanged were the steel chain-link fence and the security officers, though now they wore facial masks in a security booth. They greeted me cordially then requested my reason for visiting which I proudly announced that I was a former student decades ago and needed to obtain researched information for a college assignment of the school's growth and developments over the years. One security officer instructed me to wait as the other went to make inquiries in the administration office.

While waiting, I gazed around the quiet compound, which was visibly absent of students due to the pandemic. It was surreal as I had flashbacks of myself in my school uniform playing, running, and eating my lunch. I attempted to suck up every second of time while on the campus, cognizant of the reality that my feet might never again stroll these sacred grounds.

Surprisingly, the two one-story classrooms had been demolished and replaced with a newly paved asphalt parking lot with new model parked vehicles and beautifully colorful assorted plants and trees.

While socially self-distancing, I was cordially greeted by one of the teachers, Ms. Rolle, who apologized for the absence of the principal. I was informed that in terms of a new development, Naomi Blatch Primary School was no longer a primary school, but on November 24, 2014, it had been re-graded as a preschool! “Wow!” I reacted!

Naomi Blatch Pre-school (Formerly Primary School)
Photo taken by Photographer Ahvia Campbell
Used with permission, Ministry of Education
Nassau, Bahamas

I was very excited about this new and major development because I had never attended a preschool, so I considered this a plus for this community. Bahamas Press (2014) cited the then current Minister of Education Science and Technology, the Honorable Jerome K. Fitzgerald during Naomi Blatch Preschool’s re-grading ceremony on the 24 November,

2014 stating, *"Today is a testament of the priority of education at all levels. Both the Ministry and Department of Education have placed a high value on early childhood education and have made it of utmost importance to ensure that preschoolers receive a quality education that truly prepares them for grade school."*

Fitzgerald went on to state that the Ministry of Education new upgrades were necessary to create the safe learning environment necessary for students to thrive. He emphasized that the Ministry was deliberate in its design strategy to ensure that the facilities were indeed age-appropriate. He verified the huge financial investment to upgrade this facility for construction, repairs, and the replacement of furniture supplies to meet preschool standards.

Desks, chairs, and all other classroom furniture had to be changed to accommodate the preschoolers. The upper level was renovated to house the principal's office, a classroom was transformed into a staff room, and a resource room was created. Bathrooms were completely remodeled and outfitted with toddler-sized toilets and lower sinks to allow ease of use for preschoolers, so plumbing was updated, as well as electrical work. A playground was retrofitted, and a boundary wall was constructed and a security booth installed to ensure everyone's safety.

Minister Fitzgerald explained that, Naomi Blatch Primary School students were amalgamated with the T.G. Glover Primary School students, which created an opportunity for a much-needed preschool in this area. He pleaded for people to, *"continue to ensure that all steps in the education ladder are securely positioned so that our children can climb to the top and have every possible opportunity to succeed."*

Minister Fitzgerald wished the principal, teachers, and students the best in their future endeavors, then challenged them to maintain this great institution's reputation: "May the Naomi Blatch Preschool exceed expectations!"

I learnt from Ms. Rolle that the school's population totaled seventy students. She showed me a room the principal had dedicated for chapel services. I viewed the outdoors and playground refurbished with new preschool outdoor equipment, toys, and a new gravel playing field. Ms. Rolle described the various new online virtual programs the school had adopted in the wake of the pandemic.

Another highlight of Naomi Blatch Preschool was documented by Embri Stuart-Kamau in Bahamas Information Services (2017) when about sixty pre-school students their Principal as well as teachers visited the Police Headquarters, Fire Services Division. The group learned about fire safety and the fire station's functions, rode fire engines, and even made a courtesy call to the Commissioner of Police. Exercises were conducted on the importance of smoke detectors, use of the emergency number 911 or 919, and how best to react in the case of a fire. The children were able to demonstrate the 'stop, drop and roll' technique that should be used if their clothes have caught on fire. I congratulate the Naomi Blatch Preschool for such an excellent educational experience.

YouTube (2013) displayed Naomi Blatch Preschool students participating in a costume parade at the conclusion of Preschool Week. I visualized some very young and excited students beautifully adorned in colorful designed junkanoo costumes dancing, beating drums, blowing whistles, and shaking cowbells. As an alumna, I was truly impressed with the preschool's cultural growth and developments.

ZNS Network (2017) televised the opening of the preschool's modernized computer lab. A bank official reported that her financial institution adjacent to the school, in conjunction with a paper company, facilitated such an initiative. She enthusiastically mentioned a new library room, a children's reading room, and donations of physical-education uniforms, books, and school supplies for each child. The principal was elated and grateful because this had been a long-term vision of hers. She asserted that these new facilities would enrich the students' numeracy, literacy, and cognitive skills.

Based on my observation, my alma mater's strong academic legacy continues to develop and expand. I am honored and privileged to have attended Naomi Blatch Primary School with such a rich history, innovative functionality, and optimistic futuristic outlook.

Historically according to the Bahamas National Archives (n.d.), the school's patron, Mrs. Naomi Irene Richardson Blatch, was the youngest of the late Mr. and Mrs. Nathaniel Richardson's ten children. She was transferred to St. Francis Xavier's School, where she had an influential teacher in the person of Sister Helen Mary and it was here that she was really inspired to become an educator. In June 1927, she was valedictorian of her class.

The following September, Naomi Blatch became a Grade One Pupil Teacher at the Quarry Mission School and eventually a supervisor of Grade Three, then Grade Four, also assisted with Music at the piano. In 1930, she was transferred to Western Senior School. From 1934 to 1938, Mrs. Blatch was head teacher of Western Preparatory. In August 1938, she was transferred to The Bluff on Eleuthera, Bahamas as its head teacher. The following year she received a scholarship to Tuskegee Institute, where she spent a year before resuming her duties at The Bluff in September 1940. In early 1942, Mrs. Blatch became First Assistant at Nassau's Southern Primary School, where she was also acting head of the school. In 1945, when Southern Senior School was founded, she was appointed First Assistant.

After passing the Professional Examination for Teachers, Mrs. Blatch was named Acting Head Teacher of Southern Preparatory III in January 1959. When the prefab building on Windsor Lane, the site of which Stephen Dillet Primary School now occupies, was completed and the children were transferred there, she kept her post as headmistress until her retirement in 1970.

Reportedly, in 1981 Mrs. Naomi Blatch was rehired and stationed at Willard Patton Primary School on Augusta Street, where she taught some of her former students' grandchildren. Bahamas Archives (n.d.) highlighted;

"This grand dame of education was honored by the Bahamas Government when a local Primary School was named after her."

S. C. McPherson Junior High School
Photo taken by Photographer Ahvia Campbell
Used with permission, Ministry of Education
Nassau, Bahamas

I also had an awesome opportunity to visit my other alma mater the S. C. McPherson Junior High School. At the entrance gate a masked security officer seated in a booth inquired about the reason of my visit, next permitted me to enter. At the administrative office another security officer took my temperature and allowed me to sanitize my hands then inquired about the details of my visit. I gazed around the campus, feeling as if I were drawn into the 1970's time capsule. The front-entrance pathway was mostly unchanged except for more luscious trees and plants and a well-trimmed lawn. The building, painted in mustard-trimmed green, reflected beautifully in the sun. New two-story classrooms and a large veranda lunch area had been built.

I was informed that the student enrolment remained about one thousand and that teachers now used white promethean boards for instruction. During my visit, only a few students were on campus, wearing masks for final national examinations. I learnt from a school official in the administration office that lessons were taught virtually at this time. S. C. McPherson Junior High School continues to provide academic studies and other electives in business, entrepreneurial skills, foreign languages, arts, drama, agriculture, technical drawing, and family consumer sciences.

Bahamas Local (2010) highlighted sixteen S.C. McPherson eighth graders who had passed four Bahamas Junior Certificate examinations with mostly As. and Bs. Another Minister of Education, Science, and Technology the Honorable Desmond

Bannister and education officials congratulated them and presented them with dictionaries to assist them in their studies.

Bahamas Local (2016) drew attention to S.C. McPherson teachers who were lauded for good school leadership by the Minister of Education, Science and Technology the Honorable Jerome K. Fitzgerald stating that the institution, *"has the honor of being one of the schools in the Southwestern district that is a part of the pilot programme of the Four Disciplines of Execution (4DX)."* He praised the teachers for their commitment to the teaching profession and for their students' top performance on the Bahamas Junior Certificate examinations. Minister Fitzgerald asserted that S.C. McPherson continued to improve each year and maintained the highest numbers of A-to-C and A-to-D passes among public schools. He noted that it exemplified what can be accomplished through a strong partnership of all stakeholders: "S. C. is a shining example of how students who are prepared to learn, parents who are supportive, teachers who are committed, and administrators who have the dedication and heart to lead continue to produce some outstanding results, so I congratulate you."

I am indeed very impressed with the high standards of excellence my alma mater continues to achieve even higher. Today for me was once again a confirmation of Barbie's golden oldie: *"Unforgettable!"*

The S. C. McPherson Junior High School has a fascinating history as well. According to its Student Handbook (n.d.), Mr. Samuel Conrad McPherson, its namesake, was born in Eight Mile Rock, Grand Bahama, on May 13, 1886, to John Franklyn and Phyllis McPherson (*née Grant*). At the age of six months, he returned with his family to Nassau, where his father re-joined the police force and Samuel enrolled in the Boys Central School, Nassau Court. As a young man he worked as a tailor's apprentice before migrating to Miami, where he impressed his superiors at Burdines with his sewing skills and was a tailor for sixty years. The influence of Samuel Conrad McPherson's involvement in the Universal Negro Improvement Association spurred him to encourage Bahamians to better themselves. To that end he formed the Working Women's Wheel.

McPherson was married to Muriel Brewster of Barbados, and they had two children. As a Member of Parliament, Samuel Conrad McPherson served for two terms for "Over-the-Hill" New Providence in 1923. In 1925, McPherson Street off Market Street was named in his honor. In 1927, he helped to defeat the proposal for closing the government high school known as "Old Boys Central School." Samuel Conrad McPherson died on July 20, 1972, at age eighty-six. However, his memory lives on in the halls of S.C. McPherson Junior High School, which was founded in August 1972.

The school is located on Baillou Hill Road near Carmichael Road on the original site of the old Jordan Prince William School, which at that time enrolled junior and senior high-school students. S.C. McPherson School moved to this location in August 1974 and became a junior high school. By 1990 it had completed a three-year conversion into a secondary school, though it is now a junior high school again. It is unique as one of the few government schools to house a deaf unit at that time. S. C. McPherson Junior High School's motto is **"Love, Life, Peace, and Understanding,"** and its slogan is **"Only the**

Best is Good Enough." I can substantiate that these words are true.

The A. F. Adderley Junior High School (Formerly Senior High School). Photo taken by Photographer Ahvia Campbell
Used with permission, Ministry of Education
Nassau, Bahamas

My final visit for that day was to my final alma mater A. F. Adderley Senior High School, surprisingly now a junior high school for grades seven to nine. Except the gymnasium, all previous school rooms were demolished and replaced by a newly built two-story concrete structured building with numerous classrooms painted mustard-trimmed green.

I had the awesome opportunity to interview the school's current principal who verified that about ten years ago the old buildings had to be gutted to accommodate its new uses. In 1977 the school operated junior-and senior-level campuses. Major new developments include two computer labs, a library, a family life course, an agriculture program, Spanish and French Languages, Business Entrepreneurial classes. The existing student enrolment is about nine hundred and twenty with the possibility of an increase in the future.

Prior to the COVID-19 a New Unit program commenced for children diagnosed with Attention Deficit Hyperactivity Disorder (ADHD), as well as other disabilities; one student uses a wheelchair. The Teachers Unit routinely evaluates the small number of students to ensure the effectiveness of instruction and a workable teacher-to-student ratio.

A few years ago, a fellow alumna invited me to a meeting where a passionate plea was made for volunteers to assist in our sponsored reading program at A. F. Adderley Junior High School. Compelled to serve I volunteered to assist. I considered the reading program to be the most rewarding, fulfilling, joyful, and impactful of all our efforts. As volunteers we met one to two days weekly with academic challenged students to assist them in improving their writing and reading skills. We also taught students about personal hygiene, grooming, character skills, and the significance of education.

I concluded that our roles as volunteers proved to be a strong motivating and positive influence for the students. We demonstrated great patience and when necessary, an authoritative voice for them to believe in themselves and work tediously to achieve academic success, thereby to function effectively in a modern, educated, and technological world.

At the end of a school year our alumni group hosted an awards ceremony and social event. Along with the administrative and guidance departments staff we all beamed with overwhelming joy and pride as several students' GPA scores increased, while others read with more fluency. Students who made minimal progress were also praised for their efforts, but encouraged to work harder. (We only recently ceased our sessions due to the COVID 19 pandemic.)

Because A.F. Adderley High School invested so much in me holistically, I wanted to return to assist my alma mater in some tangible ways. It was my way simply of saying, "Thank you, Tiger Country!"

The A.F. Adderley High School Student Handbook (n.d.) cited that the school, originally named Southern Senior School, was on the corner of Wulff Road and Collins Avenue in the building that now houses Columbus Primary School. A. F. Adderley began as a secondary school where students wrote the Cambridge Junior Certificate examination to conclude their secondary-school education. In 1966, the school was moved to its present site on the corner of Harold and Balliou Hill roads and renamed the Harold Road Secondary School, which was changed to Baillou Hill High. In 1973 the name was changed again to the A. F. Adderley Secondary School in honor of the late Alfred Francis Adderley, who was dubbed Commander of the Most Excellent Order of the British Empire because of his contribution to Bahamian society in law, education, sports, politics, and government.

Bahamas National Archives (n.d.) documented that Alfred Francis Adderley was born in Nassau on November 16, 1891, as the son of Mr. Wilfred and Letitia Eliza McMinn Adderley. He attended Boys Central School and the Nassau Grammar School until 1908, when he entered Denstone College, Staffordshire, England. He worked in New York City for a year to finance his education. In 1912 he entered St. Catherine's College, Cambridge, earning B.A. and LL.B. degrees with honors.

Adderley returned to the Bahamas to practice law and was called to the Bahamas Bar in August 1919. In 1923 he was elected to the House of Assembly for Eleuthera, Bahamas and in 1928 he returned to the Western District. He married Ethel Millicent Louise Lunn on April 29, 1925, and fathered two sons: Dr. Francis E. Adderley and the Honourable Paul L. Adderley, former Minister of Finance, Minister of External Affairs, Education, Culture, and Attorney General. The former Harold Road High School, renamed Baillou Hill Road High in

1973, was renamed the A.F. Adderley High School to acknowledge his contributions to Bahamian Society.

Personally, it was truly an unforgettable experience for me to be alive to visually assess the awesome growth and developments my former schools had undergone, especially during this modern advanced technological era, to enhance students educationally in more intriguing, transformative, revolutionary ways. All I can say is, "Wow!"

Chapter 9
Poem: My Favorite Teacher Ms. Inspiration

My favorite teacher is Ms. Inspiration
When she steps into our classroom
Get ready it's an academic revolution!
Classmates: quickly buckle up in your seats
Get ready for turbulent old fashion,
Cutting-edge teaching techniques.

Ms. Inspiration is a powerful magnetic influence,
Plus an explosive dynamite of supreme motivation!
Beautiful outwardly, inwardly
Don't underestimate, or be fooled
By her exterior mask.
She's an extraordinary gifted
Educator with a soft heart.

Ms. Inspiration is an eloquent scholarly orator
When she speaks you'd believe
Possibly a Yale, or Harvard professor.
A walking historian
World history flows in her blood, as well as
Intellectual words flow effortlessly from her mouth.

Every class time was a shock and awe
As Ms. Inspiration spewed out complex subjects
Next, masterfully dissected them all!
She erupts volcanic outflows of wisdom,
Knowledge far beyond her controls.
For hours I stared transfixed as Ms. Inspiration
Proficiently crafted her skills to create
Positive, transforming, calm classroom atmospheres.
Ms. Inspiration skillfully, injects inspiring
Words to revive young thirsty, dehydrated,
Dying uneducated lives.
I pray Ms. Inspiration's excellent teaching spirit is quickly inhaled, exhaled to push out and
Birth new passionate educationalists!
Ms. Inspiration may they emulate you and your innovative trail blazing teaching styles,

Positive character, intense passion,
Lifelong educational career paths.
To my esteem Ms. Inspiration
I proudly and boldly nominate,
Vote, crown, and sash you
"My Favorite Teacher of Every Year"
As you continue to exemplify and
Role-play the greatest Master Teacher,
Christ Jesus, one far beyond all our times.

Chapter 10
My Favorite Delicious Mouthwatering Bahamian Fruits!

Mother Mango

Once again, I was blessed to be alive and to experience the dawning of another beautiful morning.

A cool palm breeze awoke to gently caress my lovely face and blow tender kisses on my lips. Lovely bold red hibiscus flowers yawned, aroused from a deep sleep, slowly opened their large petal mouths to inhale CO_2 and then exhale O_2, to join in an early-morning hallelujah chorus of praise. I turned my head easterly as a huge eye blinding blazing yellow sun dominantly positioned itself in the eastern sky, next crept slowly like a toad upward toward the cloudless blue skies.

I only had to unlock my white front door to be greeted by dozens of mangoes on my neighbor Mr. Saunders' huge Mother Mango fruit tree. A huge branch of mangos hung legally very low in my yard as if they were free gifts, while others lay helplessly on the ground after being forcibly shaken by a strong night wind.

I stared lovingly, joyously, greedily for mangos. Biologically, when very young a mango's skin is green, and body texture firm with assorted small sized seeds. Contrastingly, when mature a mango, miraculously transforms into a lovely, brilliant, yellow skinned, larger-sized, soft texture exotic tropical fruit.

Quickly, I lifted my hands to my head as dozens of mangos joined in a tempting irresistible melodious thunderous chorus, "Come, eat, and dine, Ms. Thelma!" My tiny nose sniffed like that of a hungry Bahamian pot-cake dog in search of its meal as an intoxicating mango aroma saturated the air. Helplessly, I fell gullibly for Mother Mango's attractive, graving, tempting stomach-growling appetizing desires.

Greedily, I picked and stripped a mango of its firm yellow skin with my teeth, then bit firmly into its soft yellow flesh. Next, I chewed the mango around in my mouth, and swallowed her. "Oh, my gosh!" I exclaimed as the mango tasted tantalizing, delicious, delectable, chewy, yum, yum, yummy! It was mouthwatering, sweet, succulent, and soft as it melted in my mouth. At the moment I was enraptured, eclipsed unaware of time, place, or events.

I recalled, when I was a child, yellow liquid mango juices drained downward on both sides of my mouth, hands, and elbows, then shockingly stained my aqua-and-white-checkered blouse and my beautiful aqua school jumper. Unfortunately, those stains were very difficult to remove. Though fearful of being scolded by my mother, I resolved to suffer such a tiny consequence for the greater benefits of stomach satisfaction and, above all, healthy nutrition.

Amazingly, mangos have exceptional talents, as you can place its beautiful yellow chunks of flesh in a blender and, after less than minutes produce a purée of a thick, smooth, exotic, tropical smoothie that is organically nutritiously rich in fiber with proteins and Vitamin C. Mangos are excellent for our digestive and immune systems to sustain optimum physical health. I recalled, when I was a child, I would sit in my back yard, tip my head backward, close my eyes and open my little mouth as wide as an ocean to drink a mango juice. Its liquid is always soothing and refreshing as it slowly traveled down my throat, esophagus and stomach with a *slush, slush, slush.*

Mangos are excellent for digestive and immune systems as well. I loved it when my mother would slice and chop mangos to mix in a large bowl with other fruits such as oranges, pineapples, and bananas for an awesome, delightful, exotic tropical fruit salad. Unashamedly, I would beg my friends for mangos or would purchase it from the supermarket.

Hours later I was back outside again. I stared greedily at my neighbor Mr. Saunders' Mother Mango tree. Uncontrollably, like an obsessive addict, my hands reached for another, then another mango. Unapologetically, I could not eat only one mango, but sometimes two or three all at once! Honestly, I am ravished by Mother Mango's amazing beauty as well as delicious taste, which always exceed my preconceived expectations, and most of all, my wildest dreams!

(The author's beautiful, delicious mangos from her neighbor Mr. Saunders's Mother Mango tree.)

Simply Bananas in Love!

If you ever wore my shoes, then you would understand my feelings as to why I am madly in love, simply bananas, over bananas.

Over the years my family had only a few Mother Banana trees in our small backyard, but it was actually during the 2020 COVID-19 pandemic, due to the consistent extended lockdowns, and with tons of time on our hands, that we decided to dig the soil and plant more seeds of okras, tomatoes, plantains, and, yes, bananas!

My family's bananas are similarly purchased from a supermarket or given to us by friends, neighbors, and relatives. In my small back yard are eight medium-height banana trees planted. Some stand erect, others tilt left or right with beautiful, luscious, broad, thick, green healthy leaves dancing gracefully in the soft breeze. After months of divine intervention of sunlight, carbon dioxide, rain, and minerals from the heavenly skies including my tap water, and talking lovingly to my banana trees, they miraculously, gorgeously blossomed, developed, matured, grew!

Just one month ago, my family, sisters, sisters-in-law, and friend Mrs. Curry all reaped a bountiful harvest from my banana trees with about fifty ripe bananas on each stock. I enjoyed each morning's luxury of simply opening my back door and casually striding to cut my organic, authentic, naturally Bahamian homegrown bananas! It was as if I were shopping at a supermarket for fruits, except now I was picking the bananas in my own back yard at no cost, budget-friendly, no need to burn gasoline for transportation, and, above all, nutritious.

Some mornings I sat at my dining table for breakfast with a plate of boiled yellow grits, a tuna salad, and a cup of hot water mixed with green lime. Ecstatically pleased while beaming with great pride, I picked a single banana, then slowly peeled each side of her lovely green skin from top to bottom, revealing a short but medium-height, slender white soft marshmallow-fleshy soft fruit. I took several bites and swallowed. The banana was "amazingly, delicious!"

I gave a small stock of bananas to Mrs. Curry, whose sisters lauded her as a veteran Ms. Banana bread-baker. She agreed to bake a banana cake for my family to confirm or deny her title. Weeks later, she arrived with the banana bread! True to form, my family and I were not disappointed as the banana aroma penetrated our house. Hastily, I took a small knife and sliced a medium-sized portion of the banana bread, beautifully adorned in a golden brownish top layer. I nodded my head in approval; it tasted soft, mushy, sweet, delicious, and sumptuous! I concurred with Mrs. Curry's family that her Ms. Banana bread was off the chain, and she indeed possessed a golden baking Midas touch!

The following Saturday, my daughter Christina prepared and fried fluffy, soft, sweet Ms. Banana pancakes. She firmly pressed and mixed several ripe Ms. Bananas in a small bowl along with flour, baking powder, sugar, and water, then stirred the mixture together and fried it with oil in a hot frying pan. Ms. Banana, in my opinion, is unique because you can eat her raw, baked as a dessert, fried, or blended as a drink.

I confess that my body, stomach, and appetite are madly in love, simply bananas, over Ms. Bananas! I eat her for breakfast, lunch, dinner, or snacks. She provides healthy, nutritious benefits to my body: Vitamin C, iron, sugar, carbohydrates, magnesium, potassium, and, above all, absolutely no cholesterol or sodium. Ms. Bananas sustains my life, health, strength, and length of days on earth. Ms. Bananas are precisely what any doctor would encourage unless there are some underlining medical problems. In contrast, my physician would never hesitate to quickly scroll the word ‘Bananas’ on her prescription pad for me to take as prescribed, or whenever necessary! “Wow!”

It would indeed be remiss of me and my family, not to thank our family and friends for their conscientious efforts, agricultural advice, and enduring patience in assisting us with our fruitful, nutritious, and budget friendly home grown small back-yard garden.

The author in her small backyard garden with her lovely homegrown, organic, authentic, luscious banana plants.

Ms. Contestant Pineapple

Good evening, ladies, and gentleman, and welcome to the Crown Jewels Resort Ballroom! Applaud for contestant Ms. Pineapple all the way from Gregory Town, Eleuthera, in the Bahamas, a historical land of freedom. Ms. Pineapple is vying along with Ms. Mango and Ms. Banana for the prestigious international title of *"Ms. Thelma's Favorite Bahamian Fruit!"*

Ms. Contestant Pineapple prides herself on being cultivated in Eleuthera soil, as well as scrumptiously consumed on the island or exported throughout the Bahamas and internationally. Ms. Contestant Pineapple has a short, stocky figure with an exterior color with a mixture of green, brown, beige with streaks of black and gray, which later transforms to a golden yellow as it ripens. Ms. Pineapple was gracefully, yet elegantly adorned in a tough outer skin with a sticky top stem of multiple leaves on the crown of her head. If patiently permitted to ripen to full maturity, Ms. Contestant Pineapple usually tastes extremely sweet and succulent; if not, she will be sour. If many pineapples are consumed, they can cause stomach pain, vomiting, or nausea.

"Judges, ladies and gentlemen, when Ms. Pineapple's firm, stock body's outer skinned layer is cut off, a nude white body of white flesh is exposed!" Ms. Contestant Pineapple can be prepared raw as a delicious desert or placed in conch salad, pie fillings, or toppings for cheese and pineapple upside-down cakes. "Ladies and gentlemen, Ms. Pineapple is healthy, high fiber, excellent to assist with food digestion!" Her nutrients are calcium, manganese, folic acid, and Vitamins A and C. Just eating only a few slices of her can instantly boost your immune system, energy levels, and hair, nail, and teeth growth. "Wow! Judges, ladies, and gentlemen, although Ms. Pineapple is seasonal, Ms. Thelma has no problem patiently waiting each year for due season or freezes it!"

After a pin-dropping silence, a distinguished judge announced a painstaking final decision of the results: "Ladies and gentlemen, the winner of Ms. Thelma's Favorite Bahamian Fruits are stunningly, collectively, Ms. Contestant Pineapple, Ms. Mango, *and* Ms. Banana, because Ms. Thelma loves them all passionately and equally! They are all nutritiously vital to Ms. Thelma's physical health, but more importantly, to sustain a long, enjoyable memorable life with family and friends, never forgetting to create "Unforgettable Memories."

Pineapples from the Pineapple Fields of Gregory Town, Eleuthera, the Bahamas, cited from Bahamas Geotourism.com (2023) in association with National Geographic.

Chapter 11
My Namesake

I believe that, in every culture and nation, the word *'mother'* is beloved and cherished. No relationship is more significant in the life of a child than that of a mother and father. Their unconditional love, influence, and training prepare a child for a productive life and future.

Many young children, including teenagers, love to admire or emulate famous movie stars, hip-hop artists, as well as athletes, sometimes neglecting to recognize and appreciate their parents for their value and remarkable contributions.

I thank God for my mother and the crucial impact she has made in my life. I am forever grateful for the numerous sacrifices she made for me and our family, selflessly neglecting herself many times. My mother ensured that

I attended school and church regularly, though she was unable to attend, having to work many times on weekends at a hotel as a housekeeper. My mother is my inspiration and highly respected role model. I admire her commitment to excellence and hard work. I recall vividly when in the early mornings she would stand at the bus stop to go to work to financially support our family.

I watched with amazement how, without a college degree in economics, but common sense, wisdom, prudence, and discipline in saving her monies, participating in a financial pool called 'asue' combined with her reliance on God and ethical work standards was able financially support and care for her family. I heard my mother on several occasions arguing with a dishonest contractor. Not a quitter, I watched in awe as she diligently searched until she found an honest contractor who completed our nine-room home! At the age of eighty-six, my mother was spreading her sheets neatly on her bed every morning.

I admire my mother's great faith, strength, and resilience; she experienced many medical conditions and hospitalizations, but persevered through them all. She thereby inspired me to overcome any challenges or difficulties in my personal life. I am overwhelmingly appreciative of the good example, training and counsel my mother gave me from my childhood into my adulthood. I loved that my mother permitted and encouraged me to read books quietly in my room for hours.

When I was nineteen, she gave me wise instructions on purchasing my first new car and arranged bank transactions for a loan to purchase a home. After my marriage, my husband and I constructed our new home on the exact property in which we have resided for the past thirty years. My remarkable mother made me believe I could do anything I set my mind to accomplish.

She was also very humorous and loved to make people laugh while she remained expressionless. When we visited the clinic for her routine doctor's evaluation she would have conversations with strangers and within minutes everyone in the sitting lodge would laugh hilariously at her jokes. Interestingly, as an adult, I have become more humorous and have emulated many of her positive character traits.

I believe we can never adequately repay our mothers for their unceasing prayers, unconditional and unselfish love, sacrifices and physical labors. I am thankful for my mother's perseverance during pregnancy with its many discomforts, intense labor, and my birth. The many sleepless nights caring for us when we were either sick or hospitalized; wiping our feverish brows; changing our diapers; assisting us with homework; purchasing our school supplies; transporting us to school or walking us to the bus stop while listening to our problems; never going to sleep until we were safely indoors; etc. Mothers are always busy cooking, cleaning, working, and caring for their families. While resting from their work, their minds and hearts are reflecting on us.

My mother was an amazing cook! The music to my ears were the loud orchestra sounds of *clang, bang, and boom* from pots and pans whenever she was cooking or baking in the kitchen. She looked similar to a professional cook adorned in her white apron. I laughed at her comical facial expressions after she tasted the different pots, one minute she frowned, the next minute she smiled then finally nodded repeatedly in approval. Within an hour the tantalizing aroma could be smelt thorough out the entire house. Sometimes, I watched as my mother prepared guava duff by kneading the dough then placed the pealed sliced guava inside, following wrapped it tightly in a cloth then placed in a hot pot of water to boil for hours until cooked. Next she instructed me to assist in preparing the guava sauce. When completed this Bahamian dessert was unbelievably delicious! My mother's sumptuous peas and rice, barbeque chicken, macaroni, and cheese, stemmed grouper fish, and potatoes salad were definitely of the chain. Of course, Barbie was left in charge with instructions as to when everyone could eat after mother went to work. I resolved to submit to Barbie's authority and patiently waited in great expectation of eating the sumptuous meal.

Many times we take our mothers for granted and neglect or abandon them in later years. If your mother is alive, make a concerted effort to write or verbally express your appreciation for her, give her a call, visit her, or demonstrate some act of kindness toward her. If your mother was not involved in your life, a negative influence, or a poor example, ask God to remove the anger, hatred, and bitterness from your heart, forgive her, and then strive to be a better person and a greater parent than she was. If for no other reason, give God thanks for your mother and father reproducing and giving birth to you and the blessing of the precious gift of life. If your mother is deceased, value the lessons she taught you, treasure her precious memories in your mind, heart, and soul; next, seek to follow in her exemplary footsteps.

My mother always advised my siblings and me not to worry about her because God was with her. As she continued to aged it was an immense joy, privilege, and humbly experience for me and my siblings to assist in transporting her to the bank, doctor visits, and supermarket, push her in the wheel chair, assist in preparing her meals, assist with her baths, and later employed a care-taker to assist in her daily care.

At age 88 on Tuesday, December 12, 2017, my darling mother, Mrs. Thelma, transitioned from earthly time into eternity. Her memorable life left a void, nevertheless a legacy of unconditional love, untiring dedication, resilience, and loyalty to our family, community, and nation. With great faith and hope, I anticipate seeing my beloved mother, again in heaven. This faith, hope, and expectation is what propels me forward each day and the ability to live with great comfort, peace, joy, courage, determination, but above and all, always carry in my heart her precious unforgettable memories.

Author and her mother

Chapter 12
Poem: I Wore My Pearls Today!

To all my critics!
To all my naysayers!
To all my doubters!
To all my mockers!
To all my haters!
To all my dream-killers!
Yes! Open your stunned, wide black,
Brown, blue, gray, green, hazel eyes.
Guess what?
I wore my exquisite, classy pearls today!

From your nonstop verbal abuses,
negativities, slanders,
Lies, gossip whispered also deafeningly
spoken about me.
From your graveside burial last rites of my
dreams
Dusted then blatantly trampled, trodden on
me.

Well, I boldly interrupt
Your disparaging private memorial service
Now in session for me,
To courageously announce that I am validated
Therefore, I wore my exquisite, classy pearls today!

Wow! Dazzling! Brilliant eye-blinding gems, aren't they?
Majestic, magnificent, lovely, elegant jewels
Be-jeweled on me!
My lovely pearl earrings celebrate with hand clapping
Jubilant, victorious praises
While, my high neckline pearls
Boldly choked me to sing,
Loud foot stomping, "thud, thud,"
Hallelujahs of continuous praises
To my Divine King.

Yes! Open your stunned wide black,
Brown, blue, gray, green, hazel eyes.
Come even closer,
Look, behold and see
How I'm decked out today in my dazzling precious
Coronation regalia ceremoniously beautified on me.

I'm gifted beyond measure.
I deserve it, it's mine.
A rich inheritance to be queenly adorned
In God's stupendous, radiant, picturesque, glorious awe.

To all my supporters!
To all my optimists!
To all my devotees!
To all my motivators!
To all my vision-builders!
To all my followers!
Yes! Open your stunned wide black,
Brown, blue, gray, green, hazel eyes.
Come even closer,
Look behold and see.
It is indeed a destined befitting occasion for me
To daringly announce, that I wore my pearls today!

(View a live recording of author reciting poem ***"I Wore My Pearls Today"*** On YouTube.)

Chapter 13
Poem: My Sign of Hope

Amid gross darkness in an evil chaotic world
Child abuse, assaults, stabbings, shootings,
Rapes, domestic violence, murders,
Local and international terrors won't stop
Climbing to roof-tops.
Coldhearted and mercilessly
Striking, fighting, bruising, wounding
Tragically killing to our deepest core!
Shamelessly no fear, no respect,
no reverence for man, beast, or God
Shockingly, bright red blood splattered on
Walls, windows, doors, floors, streets;
Hollering, weeping, pleading, asking,
"Why, why, why me?"

Families, societies in excruciating pains and griefs
Crying helplessly, hoping desperately
For quick healing and relief!

I collapse on my knees, bow my head
In desperate search of my only sign of hope.
Oh God, shine on me to arise vanishing
The gloominess in and outside.
Next, snuggle me tightly in Your loving,
Massive, majestic, glorious warm embrace
to patiently, wait
Until the storms of life blows by clearing
the chaos, shame, and disgrace
To create mutual harmony, perfect peace,
agape love
Ecstatic joy, and abundant grace.

Chapter 14
Achieving Optimum Success

Without a doubt time is off the essence, as it waits for no one. Each day with the tick of the clock, *tick, tock, tick, tock,* time is cut shorter, while procrastination, complacency, excuses, evil, and death lurks dangerously but deceptively on the outskirts of precious innocent fragile human lives, waiting to strike at any moment their most vulnerable, naïve, unwise victims.

For too long I have lain to sleep, leaving dormant my inherent gifts, talents, dreams, visions, goals, and purpose. These were all deposited and deeply embedded in the core of my body, mind, soul, and spirit by my loving, generous Creator. Tragically, my doubts, fears, complacent attitude, and excuses have produced numerous missed opportunities with no one to blame but me!

Weekly graveside mourners, adorned in black attire with grief-stricken countenances, loudly clapped their hands, stomped their feet, rocked their bodies, and sang melodious funeral songs as religious officiants pronounce last rites stating, "Ashes to ashes, dust to dust" on the caskets of numerous persons' God-given prophetic dreams, visions, goals, purposes, and destinies!

Loud shrieking screams are heard as caskets are slowly lowered six feet deep into Mother Earth and doused with holy water!

I concluded that if we do the things which are crucial to achieving optimum success, we will succeed and experience its wonderful benefits.

I recommend our reliance on our Heavenly Father who is the source of our existence, needs, abilities, and empowerment. ***"I am the vine, and you are the branches. Those who remain in me, and I in them, will bear much fruit; for you can do nothing without me."*** (John 15:5 Good News Translation). ***"I can***

do all things through Christ who strengthens me.” (Philippians 4:13 New King James Version).

I believe the first step to failure is to leave God out of our lives and plans. ***“For I know the plans I have for you, declares the Lord, plans to prosper you and not to harm you, plans to give you hope and a future.”*** (Jeremiah 29:11 New International Version).

In my opinion, a decision and choice to rely on God is not a sign of physical weakness or a lack of intelligence. *Rather, it is reverential knowledge, understanding, wisdom, revelation, discernment, and truth.*

Our self-esteem substantiates that we are special, unique, priceless gifts sent from God in heaven to planet earth with a divine assignment. Though, there are billions of people in the world, amazingly each person possesses distinct physical features, personalities, finger print, genetics, and Deoxyribonucleic acid (DNA). If we were to search in heaven, on earth, in the oceans, or under the earth, we could never find an exact carbon copy similar to you or me! “Wow!” Every day we should marvel and value ourselves as God's most precious creations. ***"I will praise you, for I am fearfully and wonderfully made; marvelous are Your works; and that my soul knows very well."*** (Psalm 139:14 New King James Version).

Maximize the skills of effective listening, effective communication, and seek wise counsel from wise instructors. Always display a humble, receptive, and teachable attitude. ***"The wise will hear and increase their learning, and the person of understanding will acquire wise counsel and the skill (to steer his course wisely and lead others to the truth)...The (reverent) fear of the Lord (that is, worshiping Him and regarding Him as truly awesome) is the beginning and the preeminent part of knowledge (its starting point and its essence); but arrogant fools despise (skilful and godly) wisdom and instruction and self-discipline."*** (cited from Proverbs 1:5 and 7 Amplified Bible).

It's stunning what we think and the words we speak can impact significantly the outcome of our decisions, choices, and behaviors positively or negatively. Positive and negative words when spoken have powerful creative, authoritative, and influence for good or terrible. It can influence us in being optimistic or pessimistic, hence impacting our successes or failures. Often persons would love to achieve optimum successes but when they mentally think about the effort, work, time, sacrifices, monies, or resources that are necessary they prefer to remain in their comfort zone or not attempt to do anything at all.

We must possess and execute faith in God combined with confidence in ourselves, excellent work ethics, and accelerated passion similar to a tractor propel through life opposing challenges and obstacles with focus, relentless determination, energies, and courage. We must put effort, time, and conscientious work into fulfilling our visions, dreams, and goals, or if not it will remain in her our minds, dreams, on written paper, or spoken repetitively to gullible listeners. I have learnt that even though, it is great to admire or celebrate other persons' successes, we have to passionately and determinately achieve optimum successes for ourselves. Usually when something is very important to us don't we make personal sacrifices to accomplish it? Don't we spend quality time perfecting it, and direct all of our energies, skills, time, finances, and resources into its successful completion? My mother often quoted these words to me, *"The ball is in your court how you bounce and throw it is controlled by you."* She meant I had choices and was ultimately responsible for determining whether to settle for mediocrity, advance forward, regress backward, remain at a standstill, or not do anything at all.

Thankfully, after the passing of time, I came to my senses. I was determined to move forward to fulfill my divine assignments on planet earth. My steadfast faith, hope in God and in His promises, my resurrection by the Holy Spirit with renewed physical energies, courage, boldness, and expectation within every fiber of my being, empowered me to arise and execute action to my dreams, visions, goals, purpose, and destiny. My driving passion and vision was to write and publish my memoir, *"Unforgettable Memories"* including the publishing and releasing of a YouTube video of my favorite poem, *"I Wore My Pearls Today."* Despite experiencing many disappointments and challenges for the past few years I was relentless, focus, determined, optimistic, hopeful, and believed that eventually I would succeed and I did with God's help, and the love and support of people who believed in me! I frequently reminded myself that a delay was not a denial and that at the prophetic timing of God it shall come to reality.

I am privileged and thrilled to have you reading the pages of my book and to share in the victorious resurrection of my dreams, visions, goals, purpose, and destiny now a reality!

Always remember that the victorious resurrection of your dreams, visions, goals, purpose, and destiny can also become a reality to create your personal unforgettable memories!

Bibliography

John 15:5 Good News Translation

Philippians 4:13 New King James Version

Jeremiah 29:11 New International Version

Psalm 139:14 New King James Version

Proverbs 1:5 & 7 Amplified Bible

Sources

Bahamas Local; (2010).
Sixteen S.C. McPherson teachers make history in education. Retrieved from https://www.bahamaslocal.com/newsitem/10112/Sixteen_S_C_McPherson_Students_make_history_in_education.html

Bahamas Local; (2016).
Teachers at S.C. McPherson praised by Minister Fitzgerald. Retrieved from https://www.bahamaslocal.com/newsitem/159239/Teachers_at_SC_McPherson_praised_by_Minister_Fitzgerald_for_good_school_leadership.html

Bahamas National Archives; (n.d.).
Alfred Adderley Bahamian educators. Retrieved from; https://www.bahamasnationalarchives.bs/assets/alfred-adderley.pdf

Bahamas National Archives; (n.d.).
Naomi Irene Blatch Bahamian educators. Retrieved from http://www.bahamasnationalarchives.bs/assets/naomi-blatch.pdf

Bahamas Press; (2014).
Bahamas Education Minister remarks at Naomi Blatch Preschool regrading ceremony. Retrieved from https://www.bahamaspress.com/bahamas-education-minister-remarks-at-naomi-blatch-preschool-regrading-ceremony%E2%80%8F/

Department of Education; (n.d.).
S.C. McPherson Junior High School Student Handbook. Nassau, BAH: Government Printing Department.

Gordon, I. (2009);
Unforgettable. YouTube, uploaded by Sam Novak, January 24, 2009. Retrieved from https://www.youtube.com/watch?v=vDN5rG3wLa4

Pinterest; (no date).
Pin on I Love. Lunch Prayer. Lisa Lou. https://www.pinterest.com/pin/261279215855376162/

Lyrics Box. (2021);
Eddie Minnis lyrics "Naughty Johnny," Lyrics Box. Retrieved from https://www.lyricsbox.com/eddie-minnis-naughty-johnny-lyrics-f6cd434. html

Bahamas Geotourism.com; (2023);
The Pineapple Fields of Gregory Town The Bahamas. Bahamas Family Islands Geotourism Program. Developed in association with National Geographic. Retrieved from https://bahamasgeotourism.com/entries/the-pineapple-fields-of-gregory-town/2c13e459-73ae-495c-a24f-8c3e3e78ca51

The Bahamas Weekly.com; (2017).
Naomi Blatch Pre-School visits Police Headquarters–Fire Services Division. Kamau, Stuart Embri. Naomi Blatch Pre-School visits Police Headquarters–Fire Services Division. http://www.thebahamasweekly.com/publish/bis-news-updates/Naomi_Blatch_Pre-School_Visits_Police_Headquarters_-_Fire_Services_Division52285.shtml

Williams, J; (2013).
Naomi Blatch Preschool. YouTube, uploaded by Janet Williams, April 28, 2013. Retrieved from https://www.youtube.com/watcv=Q47z5aYHszU&t=24s

ZNS Network; (2017).
Naomi Blatch Primary School new computer lab. YouTube, uploaded by ZNS Network, September 4, 2017. Retrieved from https://www.youtube.com/watch?v=AwU5s8NQAiw

For further copies, or to contact the author for bookings, please email her at: twbookings@hotmail.com

Prayer to Receive God's Free Gift of Abundant & Eternal Life

Dear friend, I extend to you a divine invitation for you to be a part of the family of God and enjoy the awesome and abundant life that God desires for you now on earth. He loves you so much and wants you so much. There is nothing good that we do that can make us righteous. We need God because of our sinful nature. Thankfully, the Great and Loving God, seeing our dilemma sent His Son, the Lord Jesus Christ to pay the price for our sins with His holy precious blood. We were redeemed and now able to have a personal relationship with Him.

John 3:16 states,
"For God so loved the world, that He gave His only begotten Son, that whosoever believeth in Him, should not perish, but have everlasting life."

Jesus Christ, God's Son is our Mediator and the only way to God the Father (John 14:6).

Through His death, burial, and resurrection, He provided salvation from sin and newness of life. He desires that we have abundant life and eternal life, overflowing with His goodness. Look at how He describes what He wants to give us.

John 10: 10 (AMPC)
"The thief comes only in order to steal and kill and destroy. I came that they may have and enjoy life, and have it in abundance (to the full, till it overflows)."

To receive God's gift of eternal life and become a part of His family, pray this prayer with faith in Him:

Oh God in heaven, I come to you in the name of your Son, the Lord Jesus Christ. Your Word declares that the person who comes to you, you will not cast away (John 6:37. I believe Jesus died for me and shed His precious and holy blood to wash away my sins. I believe that You raised Him from the dead. Right now, I receive Jesus Christ as my Lord and personal Savior. Father, You said in Your Word that if I do this I would be saved (Romans 10:9-10). So I now confess and boldly declare, according to God's Word, I am saved. I am born again spiritually. I am a child of God (John 1:12).

Thank You Father for receiving me, saving me, and making me a new creation in Christ Jesus (2 Corinthians 5:17).

Fill me with Your precious Holy Spirit. Empower and help me to live this life for You. In Jesus Name I pray, amen!

Made in the USA
Las Vegas, NV
09 November 2023

80541235R00066